What Kind

Wesleyan Poetry

Also by Martha Zweig

Vinegar Bone

Powers

WHAT KIND

poems

MARTHA ZWEIG

Wesleyan University Press

Middletown, Connecticut

Published by Wesleyan University Press, Middletown, CT 06459

Printed in the United States of America

5 4 3 2 1

Library of Congress Cataloging-in-Publication Data
Zweig, Martha
  What kind : poems / Martha Zweig.
      p. cm. — (Wesleyan poetry)
  ISBN 0-8195-6625-X (alk. paper) — ISBN 0-8195-6626-8 (pbk.: alk.
paper)
  I. Title. II. Series.
  PS 3576.W37 W47 2003
  811'.54 — dc21   2002156142

Contents

III. Companion Animal

IV. Shiver

Acknowledgments

Poems in this collection, some in slightly different form, have appeared elsewhere as follows:

American Literary Review, "Suspicious Bones"; *Barrow Street*, "Autumnal"; *The Black Warrior Review*, "Invective" and "Riddance"; *Boston Review*, "Spared"; *The Bridge*, "Cow Dream With Commentary"; *Carolina Quarterly*, "Moths" and "Not Mowing"; *Cincinnati Poetry Review*, "Indulging Agnes"; *Columbia: A Journal of Literature and Art*, "Ducks"; *Confluence*, "An Extra Child"; *The Connecticut Poetry Review*, "Hill Custody"; *Crazyhorse*, "Abandon" and "Flickers"; *CutBank*, "The Windhorse"; *Field: Contemporary Poetry and Poetics*, "Widowwalk" and "Dissociative"; *Green Mountains Review*, "Successor" and "Bestial"; *The Journal*, "Boughbreak"; *The Laurel Review*, "All Souls" and "Appreciative"; *New Collage*, "Baby Head"; *New Orleans Review*, "Nimbus" and "Anonym"; *The North American Review*, "Palimpsest: The Summer Cottage"; *Northwest Review*, "Cosmos," "Stay," and "Peter, Grown Up"; *One Art*, "Ward's Field" and "This Work"; *Ploughshares*, "False Memory"; *Printed Matter* (Japan), "Good Night's Sleep" (reprint, forthcoming); *Quarterly West*, "Welcome" and "Good Night's Sleep" (original publication); *Raven*, "Horses"; *Sonora Review*, "Between Floors"; *South Coast Poetry Journal*, "Scarecrow"; *tap root*, "Cosmos"; *Willow Review*, "Approach"; *The Worcester Review*, "All Souls."

"Revisitor" was first published in *The Bellingham Review;* "Rosa at Mischief" was first published in *Berkeley Poetry Review*, issue 33, winter 2002; "Snake Death" was reprinted from *The Carleton Miscellany*, copyright © March 11, 1974 by Carleton College; "City Lot" originally appeared in *The Centennial Review*, vol. XVII, no. 2, 1973, published by Michigan State University Press; "Woolen Wolves" originally appeared in *Fellowship* (April 1974), the magazine of the Fellowship of Reconciliation; "January Domestic" is reprinted from vol. 4, no. 1 of *Literary Imagination: The Review of the Association of Literary Scholars and Critics*, copyright © 2002, used by permission of The Association of Literary

Scholars and Critics; "The Fitting" and "Scraps" first appeared in the summer 2001 issue of *The Literary Review;* "Extinct" and "Envoy" first appeared in *Manoa;* "Caul" and "Rapture" were first published in *Nimrod International Journal,* vol. 41 (2), "A Range of Light: The Americas"; "Animals Burning" and "Thanksgiving" were reprinted from *Prairie Schooner* by permission of the University of Nebraska Press, copyright © 1973 and 2000, respectively, by the University of Nebraska Press; "Fleshpot" was previously published in *Sojourner: The Women's Forum,* vol. 20, no. 1 (Sept. 1994); "His Early Walk," "Primordial," and "Tenant" were originally printed in *Sou'wester;* "Porcupine" and "Ward's Field" first appeared in *The Gettysburg Review,* vol. 11, no. 3 and vol. 7, no. 3, respectively, and are reprinted here with the acknowledgment of the editors.

The Vermont Arts Council published the author's chapbook, *Powers,* which included "Baby Head," "Moths," "She Says She Dug Up Her Dead Child," "Snake Death," "Stay," and "Their Skins."

Manoa reprinted from *Powers* a selection including "Moths" and "Their Skins."

*

I thank:

The Bridge, which awarded "Cow Dream With Commentary" second prize in its first annual poetry contest.

The 1993 Mississippi Valley Poetry Contest, which awarded a second prize to "Virginity."

Sojourner: The Women's Forum, which has included "Fleshpot" in its forthcoming anthology, *Poetry From Sojourner.*

John Donoghue, Muriel Nelson, and Mark Solomon.

Agha Shahid Ali; Reginald Gibbons; Tom Lux; Heather McHugh, Steve Orlen, and the Warren Wilson MFA Program in Poetry.

The Vermont Studio Center.

The Mrs. Giles Whiting Foundation for a 1999 Writer's Award, which has helped considerably.

*

Instances of violence depicted or suggested in some of these poems are fictional.

What Kind

WELCOME

Everything here isn't harmless. The forest
requires constant charming. Firmly the toad
in the gargling roots doesn't declare
its idiom— it's up to you to catch,
in the nerves of your whole mouth, out of spontaneous
trail babble, what serviceable
spell you stumble into. How can you tell?
You'll be not yet
struck dumb.

I had a sister & she said a verse
that swung the shadows like spidermonkeys through what
little light does
trickle down. These stumps
blossomed. All of us— No. I was her favorite, that she
put the others to bed with, but O, it was she herself,
she was the lucky one! She got to sleep straight through
every freakish night— peppery
hairs!— in the very wolf's yellow breath.

I. HOT BOTTOM

THIS WORK

The cold orange hands of the
salamanders still wrap and
unwrap the baby he dreams he was
then long before there was any human family.
Then their work was just beginning on the
damp stones and mosses too.

He had to be as little strange as
possible. They were
making the world & working on him too. He
was warmer but less
strange than a moss or a stone
was, that saved him.

The moss worked on the stone too.
The stone worked
on him like a mind he
had to grow up to talk to or
dream to but without
turning strange. The

cold hands run over him.
They read the body he
dreams of as a baby's to the
stone. Before there was any
human family the work that made him was
this work just beginning.

SUSPICIOUS BONES

Mother the crutch & Daddy
the hook, I clunkered forth
a born prosthesis, or so the bones suspect.
My soul is supposed to inveigle itself
into & out of a physical
gimmick, but the bones think not.

The Disarticulator tweaks
the bones & rattles their equilibrium
out & back by the marsh, where a redwing
blackbird flares its epaulets
& shouts, & between my ears
the word for mud escapes me,

whose turtle squats & squirts
for love, & tonight ornate
yellow ladders will tread the water moonwards
off West Lake. Here the cabin sank
to the knobs & its oilcloth sills,
& stunted its front door knocker,

but the old crib woke up & did
what the waterlilies said. If your bones
afflict you, belittle them to death.
The matter gets simpler yet. It puts
the subject of the bones' abiding
distrust to rest; vindicates them.

PRIMORDIAL

A shame on her mother, the spoiled child
—slob, sourpuss, the face that froze that way— grows
up Swamp Thing. Dismay at first: hidden strange
birds blabber & from all the watery roots
kinky reflections lean up & jitter hers
too with pluck-plucking at it. Blowzy fogs
twitch by. Insects fairly screech across her hairs.

But swamp & she will take to each other.
Mushmouth, it daily swills & regurgitates
pure drivel to revel in. Luminous mud
gases tenderly bubble up her
malformative buds & little labia:
she may resort to the baggy pink orchids'
bank to nap, lick gelatinous tremella

for her treat, & for prayer may grunt froggy
in the nightly din of answers. As either
light or dark infiltrates the other, as rain
pitters through every intricacy
of the rank greenery clogged upon all
this broody dead clutter, happiness seeps
into the webs of her nerve, where she still stings.

Years' wallow! until she may think to miss
her mama who up & died, & then may pump
along, jarring from underneath them the plush
mats of engorged loosestrife & sphagnum
to dredge for mama in thick sediments

of anaerobia where things don't rot
no matter how they try, paddling the stirred-

up & resettling silt to solicit
mama out into these consolations—
one impulse vigorously asquirm inside
countless ulteriors— while her patron snakes,
who constantly memorize the loops each snag
dangles in as they travel the black limbs &
then drop, dart tiny minds in all directions.

REVISITOR

Stutter is what the rain has to say.
Of that text rain is the great speaker,
from whom hush humbly
repeats its early lessons & over
again at the gray porch, the steps
I approach in all the weathers
that turn, as they do, to rain.

A stray mind in multiples of
nuance rides the distance
home for a word where it's warm,
& where welcome prepares of itself
a leafy soup dipped after grace into bowls.
Rain fills the bowls, rain
seats me there.

Rain sings scat over the car
radio tune I accompany
with a new lyric or two. The farther
away I start from *the better*
to introduce you with my dear the
wolf said; I knew him then &
there & now: those syllables.

BETWEEN FLOORS

Mother opines, you look like
death warmed over. Sickly's
what she means, but it's just I've
fastened my evil veil on,
stuck it with its toad-
headed long hairpin
in my high bun,

& I mean to mount & descend
the stairs repeatedly, both
opposed diagonals to & from
the landing with its tall
skinny scrimmed windows,
& question the newels.
Pinch them, they'll tell:

no doubt squeak first
what matters least
in the wooden narratives —
but each time the story
increasingly nervously
knows gauzy me.
I can feel the posts flinch.

DEARLY BELOVED

Remember her? —maid-of-honor, roommate, the outsider; who
    burst
into blue blotches stifling her own objections, tipped her wicker
basket & slid the rice loose down the wedding table.
Company forked themselves pink tidbits out of a whole sockeye
    slit
& shriveled in limp salt reeds, then danced so abruptly the wine
wobbled over the goblets. Peonies arrived, but not
enough in time to crowd out the immediate family.

Bride dipped in graduated hoops under yards of light
ivory dross sprigged with snags, & when her daddy smirked
& cut in for his turn, certainly his last chance, manners
crisply tucked, bride stomped up onto his spats like his
littler girl, made her kissy face. Maid-of-honor, that instant
quite choked up, ducked out to pull at the webs reeling from
    sleeve
to sleeve around the lobby, didn't miss the spectacle any.

Couldn't've missed maid-of-honor, either, relieved,
nay, stripped of her last duties & doubling over in acute
distress later: tugged the finger-ends of her long gloves &
    removed.
Humor us? —She'd wheedled actual clergy into that
    mealymouthed
rite, booked the honeytrip straight into vagrancy, six jail cells.
Even if a travesty of hers or two flopped in the details, she stuck
a job through; at her long-suffering best she proved unforgivable.

PER STIRPES

Same identical one transaction
Daddy always offered: you'd got to want
what he'd give, not want what he wouldn't,
& so we children hurled after him
with arrows & reviled his least love.
Those days to this batter away
aimlessly the leafy grave we
shoveled him down into to an anthem.

Misfortunate man! vouch for him
he made a good money, & nighty-
nights he fatherly laid it upon our
sweet expressions— we'd each
get two bright coins on the lids
of our eyes like dead & it made
us mad, we bit air but his thumbs
stubbed us nevertheless in our beds:

Sleep tight! Rub out a dream for his pennies,
rub two together & make them do
for subtraction's remainder;
from fistful & fruitful the stipend
that furnishes this table. We sisters
snip dollies out of the folding green
currency & bellyache, while Pittance
the cat scoots us a singing cricket.

TENANT

Once she'd gone
—& took what there was of
pretty things too—
he hung up that
dirt cheap heart of his in the
narrow rib cage
to cheer him mornings,
where it hopped the little trapeze & sang like a
daughter should,
one variable trill.

Or "wife!" he sometimes
ranted, & the stuckopen transom admitted
hall noise, comings & goings & greetings,
hellos all the way up & goodbyes down.

At Halloween
fifty or more belligerent little
souls ascended.

HOME REMEDY

Bless me, cure me,
turn up another three—
baby teeth in a tiny jar

knocked down in back in the old variety drawer.
Likelier these than to pinch after the three
quarters, would it've been, I'd slip

under a boy's pillow & wonder again,
didn't I each time then? whereabouts in the wide
world a particular pocketing coin goes.

A son? Whatever possessed us?
Take me nearly a decent forgiving day's
three hours of off-&-on to find—

that's safekeeping, for you— find & then
what few dribble out on the bureau! I did
bedevil, maybe, keepsaking

the little mouth, easier said,
& maybe my split head's appreciably
relieved already,

but take these
anyhow with my glass of tea;
one, & to make it won't come back, two three.

RUMPELSTILTSKIN RECOUNTS HIS FORMATIVE YEARS

After school, I sucked up an ice-cream soda & spun the paper
    straw
into a gold one. Fingered & blew a tune on it: the trees shook
gold leaf, & usually a minor corner church in schism
clicked, took a picture: me blinking, my stained glasses.

Surprise me in the window, see myself. Birds passing notes &
    limb
from limb, stilted accentuals frequently
overdoing it, or simple suggestions that pleased me yet
I resisted, could've sworn I heard, under twitter, human snitching

to implicate me & take me down. Craw sticks & clobber stones
they chucked at me & my bones! But the everlasting unchristly
misnomers protected me: say *who*? Guess *who*? —not me, no-
body I'd ever have to stand & answer for, fill in the blank child.

ANONYM

Only naturally you yearn for your own name! so somebody
will start you one, pluck it from one of those pocket pages
the calendar displays on a yellow wall, & set it already
wriggly in its wet dish out on the sunniest sill to grow.

Meanwhile, how will you know yourself? If you must first sleep
off death, how will you return to me? Let the spruce
droop in early snow & the snow fill the county & no
track appear but fills before it gets to a door,

let the fire wallow & snuff, & still I will tuck its lights
along the bannister along the upstairs hall
to where room slowly makes up for you, & a spaciousness
prepares at the armchair; windowcurtain trembles, ruffle

to hem, & tonight I appear to myself lifting a pinch
of the fabric to one side, backlit. I forget
only the countless things, none of importance. A grudge
some loyal toolshed spider spun of the dribs & drabs

comes down one year with a single jab of the broom.
What we called you, hiding out back to be born like that.
Gagged in the billowing dust when the *corn, millet, sunflower*
seed poured into the bins, slumped sacks thicker than us girls!

And if the birds ate up what seed we scooped out to the feeders,
did it sprout? somebody small tugged, wanting to know. Who'd
think of that? Of course! as the roots grow they seize the bird
     fast—
snatch! In its birdie guts, from the inside, I confided.

ABANDON

I mention it because my mouth
clutters with dry wasps.
On bottomland my mother's other
house soaks in light seeped
from the veins of leaves,
& the vetch irreversibly winds.

Or the cloudburst we rooted for all
afternoon stumbles upon us,
roof roar absolutely frantic, din
of all the inspired names she hit on to
holler me in when I was so little I
didn't know better— I'd answer

to anything, come running: I dropped
a smashed mouse at its new hole,
dropped the rest of a bad lady's blueberry pie & dropped
my pair of her high heels someplace out in that
lush drainage gully next
to their last steps.

PETER, GROWN UP

Under my breath I could always mutter
my way into the enterprise named
one name they called me, which is: A Stone.
Say it stirred & started runny & hot: say then it
cooled down, froze
solid & that from time
to time it heaved. Over millennia
it unearthed to light.

My mother pushed me around for years in her
steep cranky uterus— version of doomed Sisyphus
she was, blowing & gasping. I didn't care.
Daddy could've taken the longsuffering
wolf's part at the three little pigs'
final impregnable house I was.
I do better. Under my breath
I always keep more breath.

Before they were little pigs I found the first two
in the sea & the last one at the bottom of the sky.
Don't be scared, I said. *You're stones*
& that is just some strange other wind that passes on.
Are you almost ready? Under my breath even an Easter
baby bunny & Easter
chick in the dead hands
always warmed to me.

FALSE MEMORY

Who'll pardon need? I was the baby &
grasped things babywise: queer smells,
voices, carpet nap all wrong. I crept
backwards, nudged rear, rolled,
sucked a red fist, knocked into & fingered at
somebody's new toy telephone, dialed up
myself the house of murder:

over there maybe fifteen tinny rings
spooked the liver-&-white
spaniel. Yelped fright twice, skidded
off tipsy, claws on floorboards,
flattened & hid itself deep beneath
the vestibule chest in nasty
dust & didn't sneeze,

& later on, hungry, the silence
long regrouped, the angle of shadows
shifted aside, same dog inched out & seemed to
veer by chance back into that room;
whined there, wriggled for shame to sniff
the tacky blood, lick it & lap: I thought so.
Mama, that part satisfied me.

SPARED

In today's permission, a dozen chickens
scratch up their little squalor together.
The yard peeps kernels. Suits me, now, these back
porch steps & across my lap a damp
tea-towel to shell the peas from: pinch
to pop a pod-seam's fat end open, then split
straight along thumbwise, & even
blindly the peas seem to tighten desperate
tiny white tails over the pot, where

were we? quick, now— brainstorm adorable
names for newborn pups before your dad
gets back! saves some, saves more than none; he'll scowl,
you kneel, point which of them is which, speak up
distinct so each particular one takes up
its particular modest prestige. O christen
before you're grown & before you bed away,
away from me, or you'll never own to your own
& proper answer, just poor twin dirt!— I missed

you but then, like the chicka chix,
a man's children & peas riot around
of no conspicuous note, & my own
name, I believe, was the name of all whatever
there is at any one time, no more farfetched
than a sledge horse's my sister
could've called out to & they followed
each other down the lost track of time
switching in the dandelion puffs.

VIRGINITY

All those
evenings cicadas
rang. *Mother I am
not here. I'm the girl in the ringing.*

    The fishes' lips
    break the top of the pond,
    say over the idle water
    ringing

        In the reed stems
        during the dark
        one fish is a clasp
        purse with one coin:

        it pays a way;
        hands
        that strung your baby limbs
        accept it.

PLAGUE

Kiss me & sooner than
otherwise you'll grow
buboes, flare up, & die of the
hocus poxes, the frog said.

Cuddlesome princess she was,
she liked to hear the pond
strum evenings. Tough stems
pushed to the top of the water

flat slit leaves, yellow topknots.
She sat with the firebugs
& chuckled over the escapades
at her window, where the glass ran

sand down for overturning
the hour, which was bedtime.
She flapped back a braid at her
confounded father, who rehearsed

prayers in his mind to make
himself kneel with difficulty.
The frog climbed up the stone,
climbed web over slab: already her

big toe stubbed, amphibian,
& as becoming to a vestigial
virgin as pink light showy under-
neath pinned-up midnight.

ROSA AT MISCHIEF

What you open is your gift.
Rosa, nine, and fire
teach each other ladylikeness,
courtesy and curls. The fire
mutters notions. Why of
all things, Rosa!
Who started it? Lurid Rosa did.
O flames, busybodies.

Whose afterlives
agitate on girl bones?
I think it is queens and chars
and bitches and bees, ices,
waters themselves. Every
one once fed earthshake:
no wonder Rosa fires
what falls to her.

All her days
when Rosa will climb her
stairsteps to bed her flames
will play up around her; some
two especially dear may catch
her hands, young
as she'll be, and old; asleep
as flamboyants ruffle around her bed—

counter- & clockwise they'll chorus,
& wrinkle & bow in orange and blue.

EXTINCT

Mother & father I once had had a child once:
she escaped in the fire. They set water
boiling momentarily, tumultuous
rolling boil, beware the pot

watched them, thought everything over,
thought harder, *mind, mind.*
So the mother picked up &
twiddled the phone, taught it to chat, while the father
steamed open his shaving mirror, & all of a sudden neither
one ever got back
to the pot, the kettle, the hot bottom of things,
& the child's
room ruffled up over the furious
kitchen stove & burned her off like a rocket crisp.

Here's how the damp black wood out back there
drudges to this day: every night it moonshines for the little girl.
Cool coals shimmer, snuff; the joists
slip & dimensions lapse to dismantle
according to the crows' step-
by-step procedure: yawk,
what ceiling? Dew,
                            brass buckle
& berry exchange.

Goodbye, then, foolish family! Who
will I love next?
Until we got so interrupted, I never
suspected anyone.

II. HAUNTS & FIGMENTS

BLASTED CANAAN

Species of tree that shirks
light rears out of the meadow. Air
sucks in the twigs & whirls. A priest,
who stopped & stayed, prayed to shift the plague
of shrivels into a stoppered crock in a dream,

& rubbed us each in the weed that worked
for sheep & for spasm
& money once, but the spell's sixth
word muttered & fouled at his lip
& the book spattered. We heard,

then, the verses of evasion
make themselves up on the spots of his tongue.
Neighbors! It behooves us to cover ourselves,
to hedge, to call the children in as if we still
might know them by given names,

& sit them to listen, however, though,
they will not, but strike out
their own way instant to next. They seize from under
the crib both sacks of the seed we shook & dragged
this far of our mothers' & fathers' fabulous yield.

BOUGHBREAK

Nobody else, only the wind tipped
up & overran the easy leaf house.
Rolled up, unrolled air. The twigs twanged
ho & hum, the notch
of the world stuck at summer,
& our mother
ticked away in her green underthings
to the sky chink the breeze got in by, twinkled
a crow's eye & spun
gone & left us slung in those lofty
groin vaults to the culminating dome of living daylights.

Tirade from the cradle!— but it falls forever. I envy
bats snug in their belfry, who burst
& pour upon dusk,
all the skin-&-bones there is
aflap upon chaos, bellowing air
over the black flames at the gorge, & then every single
one of them slips back just before dawn does, & by the time
        dawn
tugs its web up, diffuses iridescence & flattery
into the puckering faces of water & loose
limbs of the sand,
they're all tucked in.

THE FITTING

End up whether under stones or
star-studded, either way your rags
patch rags, dearie, she chats
& dismantles my dead I submit
for the dreams in their heads & in the
torques & locks of their other bones.

She permits me to watch her work,
at it still when the water wakes up
in the jar & the bread passes, take
your time, I tell her, take mine, & my
very measurements tremble
for garb, the drapes & pins, granny

fingers floating the slightest of stuffs
to settle upon me in nimblest
adjustments, while, out behind her closet,
the earth's deep unmade beds air
indefinitely, wind over them drives
what scatters, the corners accumulate.

NIMBUS

Moonlight woke me;
could've been a prowler, or
what else is the fear for?
So spoke Nance in her nightie
& headed out to the hall landing,
& there, to satisfy herself, she stomped
her slippers into the long mist

of a wedding where it slid
importantly down the stairs
in a retinue of insipid tunes
eddying from every room, hers,
too; *but I think of you all the time*
mistress of festivities, snitch
fingering in the silver—

& to clear her eyes' mind
of the linens & stains & relations
from the wrong side, strangers,
she felt back to a spigot in the bath,
certain to run either hot or cold!
If she would just turn her hand, why,
then, water would rise.

OUT-OF-BODY

Expect what else of a secretive
old woman? She harbored the crab,
kept a disorderly flesh. O please do
die out of this awful fluorescent
institution extremely soon, her suffering
visitors mumble their knuckles & croon:
those among whom her rapidly
disqualifying membership still clings.

*

When my drippings stink of the world,
I'll finger-pick up an invisible thread
to the ceiling spider. She comforts me, There-There.
Sheets then
quit your trembling, lick clean
my late bedfellow's
boxsprung bedframe's wooden sore,
slippers follow the floor away.

*

In respect of its privity, Arachne eight-
leggedly unletters the human name,
voids its vowels & strips the fricative
consonants of her dander & hair.
Strict child, evict the web.
Beverage holds the sill. Personnel
bow and plunge into surgical green gowns.
Ambivalent curtains take the air.

PALIMPSEST: THE SUMMER COTTAGE

Know her as figment glozed by a flattering light,
though she substitutes dusk for herself. She persists
here year inside the window front year out, concedes
snow to move in. Snow ravishes the glass.

Queer tremor— activates a web
near the pane she favors: it's the iced-over
lake closing in, swollen, that cracks up another
year out. Lonesome corner, too, minus its spider.

Shake out the web entirely! Did she catch in it any
mistake we two ever made worth keeping? Then she will
sweep, ameliorate the last least
flake of us sheering its way, pretty misdemeanor.

Deep thought I will not entertain of her, go: settle there.
Keep a chaste bureau in an upstairs room.
Sleep through her notice. If she wonders, offer her kinks of my
sleep, too: another derangement for her to untrouble.

AN EXTRA CHILD

Never occurs in this
family to reckon its members one
by one at table, or to speak up who'd
be who by name. I'll stay.

Chairs shift their feet
obligingly & a clear soup breathes
as gratifies itself, clinking musical spoons.
Dog wags from those knees

there over to these: I'm the another
one thing leads to, the neither
entirely unexpected, nor not. Rosy glow
upon me, timely asylum.

Pass hands: a wicker of broken bread
bears along & butter arrives, o my misdemeanor! —if salt
condescends to a pink slice
on my plate I could live to recover

the flavor of flesh I must've committed
once, was it to memory? Little doubt a presiding
adult has already mistaken me for
(it appears) my-dears-it-could've-been-

anyone, somebody we knew, & do two
of the girls (boys?) toy bits of their food half-alive
in the flicker of recognition? — o the longer I
belong here, the more I slip my mind.

ENVOY

Good girl, I will build
you a pearl in the sea & visit you there
to tell you the doings
from where I go back to live.

As often as I arrive
so will the trails of earth
from kitchen & yard of an
evening down to your ravishing shell,

one tireless plaything
you turn in. Bea mentions
pumpkins' innards, the skunks' dignity;
I said I'd remind you.

DARK SWIRL

The snow lost its bearings:
                              everything it
touched it slipped
& fell from.

High overhead in the tall street light
I picked a flake, but I missed it on its
way down.
            It missed the street.
It missed the earth.

Another time, lost soul.

ALL SOULS

I run the attic rats.
I installed the haunt here.
So far, so good: I
hold this pretty crag
for you, my innocents.

All my skinnies & fats,
cradle sweets, you want your
mother's lullaby
now, mother's hag hug.
O bonies, succulents.

Nobody dreams to you.
No twists thicken your poor
plots; your trials, lucks,
bungles & odds droop
limp in ringlets bedside,

& I'll do & undo
somewhats & whatnots for
all our days. Loves, chucks,
warbles. Snags of hope.
Fussies, hush. Be & bide.

HILL CUSTODY

Suddenly an animal will step into your
grief, a clearing:
beast with horns like the oak
trees wearing natural bells, whose green
clappers contain its families.
The sticky spiderlings ride it.
Opossums lie in its ears.
It will carry your boy on its withers
where he shines like the storytold
between two brown shoulders,
and venture the dirt trails
through cover, through starry open
from ridge to ridge of these acres.
Browser, shaggy rock-salt-licker— nobody
knows if it picks its own
infallible footing.

RAPTURE: OCTOBER, 1992

(Leaflet from the Mission for the Coming Days)

Good morning, coarse and steamy hills!
I woke up clumsy, stumbled
outright into this frost-stricken, stiff brown meadow brush
from a bitter kitchen.

Past eight! but the low-lying village cloud
still wholly occupies the pond on the common,
just where all three local
dirt roads down still bottom out.
Cloud sits, doesn't stir itself slightly
to lift off yet;
plain to tell, though, from up here,
that even pallid sunshine visibly excites it.

Flick me my daily particle,
and prepare me tomorrow's too, pips the militant chickadee
at its seed. None of a bird's business how the dog's day
today goes, or the doe's, or the skittish
human soul's. Never mind who
turns over her stew
with a dear bone,
never mind if the bowl it dribbles into carries off
faintly to some distant other supper.

Who really means it, suffering all night?
Or secondguesses to ask

whether they meant it or not, once shriven to rise?
Clean hands, dress me in the one clean wisp.

Where Shire River hooks behind municipalities
downstream, and farther down,
its rapids will nudge the mist along in and out of an evening
that decent people rely on to bless them and keep them.
The mist entertains their lights.
If good mothers
just barely touched their families at the thresholds
to bed and turned them and guided them out-of-doors
instead, and led them then to the end of human settlement,
and if they all took a couple of great
foggy breaths there,

one of them would remember me.
One of them would exclaim to another, I do believe
that someone remembers me!

Then the dee-dee-dee
hops inches into the alternative morning;
morning when, hours ago, we entered
freely into any vapor, and cleared
briskly off any water,
and nobody lives on the hills anymore because they left.
They plucked down
their houses and dismantled the town, and drift.

RIDDANCE

Lay then for Draco, lash your new tail!
The heavens sail laden
around dark barter
routes awash, flashing bravura plume
& plunge, you may roar now & fire your
tongues through the long hold.

We provincials shudder for joy to have cast off
from our seething dock that immense
weltering black boat-
bulk, golden lizard, that you turn loose
inside of & to elsewhere,
all starry ones' proper home,

& I cheer me if the vessel of your howls
clears our pilings & departs our cove
& the visible bay entirely, where now may
our own modest waters
lap in congenially again & no
familiar go brilliant.

INVECTIVE

Each dark, mockeries of June bugs knock for you,
tickle & pluck at our spring screens,
wallow after the homely lamplight
that you too fancied just such an evening in.

Let me declare my loathing at once!
Let me apprise their fabricator—
his gifts as often abominations
as not— in all his rude faces wherever

we turn that no trick of expression he owns
will move me anymore. Pinch my eye:
I will not care for any other
color to be bereft of, now, but love.

Cold comfort you, then, who are lost to us!—
even in the stars' marketplace
somebody eternal will begrudge
every scintilla you haggle for.

DISSOCIATIVE

Nearer November I forbid
courtesy & the last persistent visitors:
I make myself scarce then.
My front stoop's remaining door
answers evasively, picks at its
modest lock; meanwhile the spotless
kitchen collects its implements & amenities
& adjourns to the pond,
where silver flaps off the clanging
deciduous trees & the tumblers
lift, plates & their cups
clatter to rise
overhead into the long goose lanes.

Ah, but my domestic
featherbed plumped somewhere
upstairs sighs
in satisfaction to stay behind:
swollen with air
it consorts upon a voluminous
hush at last, where the raw moonlight loafs.

Goodbye, goodbye! There goes
the better part of my intermittent

undoing love,
shunting birds like the calculus
an abacus ticks through distance
itemizing the loss
rag by straw.
Some of that tumult carrying-on is the wind
& some is wings, the birds
in a great hurry now,
the wind hurrying after them, its
stings in tow,
scissors and its snips of snow.

WIDOWWALK

Find what's left of him derelict, ready
to rig for moonlight and the exotic flags,
now that successions of snails
lay gloss along the ribcage his pride
had once to ride in. Whitewash work
some few weeks yet, then set him sail.

Season of inflammation
in the canopy, leaves in tailspins,
augury of cargo into every bone hold
hoist and fast, bright
maple lading, the Indian pipe,
sometimes a toad,

and the pomanders of gall and balm:
accurately the rain weighs and stows.
Easy does his most intimate drudgery—
were it I so busy, belovedly;
as it is, care and courtesy
of the hired spider,

and a brisk North wind
to rabblerouse among the wild geese,
strong and splendid arrivals
who wobble our poor pond, preening
the luck from his broken hair
into their wings.

APPRECIATIVE

What did I do with that sand? O I
splurged it on pretty things
or it all turned under &
over in the waves: those
waves like ornate dresserdrawers of seething
lingerie I must always try, so
fetchingly do they dip to show it.

Gracious welcome, amiable by-the-sea,
a comfy stay. Misbehaving, I once
provoked a flap among the
gulls but none minded,
convivials of the shingle, partakers,
disreputables enjoying themselves as who
could fail to but the dead?

My hostess kept a most remarkable
domestic: even as every water
lapsed there in tatters, tide
took in the mending & scrimps & saves
everything that matters in her bag, her
kelpy scalloped hamper, her
dear sequined evening bag.

MOTHER: DIED IN HIBERNATION

Interloper daughter-bear! — is it me? but what's become
of senile legitimate Ursula who went over the mountain
in shag last fall? Whatever limp
berries she didn't positively
swat off right then I saw her simply roll over
& over in thickets of & mash flat; plugs

of wintry brain fat already crowded her flagging
charisma back into remote
random nervous feebles. Nevertheless, until April
breakup yesterday, she did dream, & so often
& artlessly of me that I reeled in her honor,
snubbed the rest of my kin, I'm told.

My own rank exhalations! —& so I have overpowered
myself out of bed & doors, privately to pursue what urgent
error of my ways? Wisps of a tepid
weathery mist start up the sensitive places rife
with trickles that register thirst soon enough, but still,
        immediately,
hunger is what really blows out the bones:

hunger that tumbled me downhill after you, once, when the
        mouth
of the world watered, before you spirited away.

CAUL

Yo, ma! how's death? I ask after her sometimes.
Welcome, or none? Ashmother, any company?
Company of which of the other creatures?

I want her to tell me what walruses
do dead, because I'm still this little: I grieve
for animals only, and grieve for all of them,
and grieve for them, as ever, inconsolably.

What I hope is that she
will thrash her way out of sin soon. Maybe then —
beasts! — she will get to be one.

Sometimes the Lords of the Dead,
who extricate and pick the whole soul
up out of my mother thinner than the hot shimmy
rising off of hearth fire in winter
evenings' chimney air,

Lords who spin her soul off
their meager fingers and wind it around
from dark to dark a while,

suddenly fling it away wide, let it fly.
It's then,
wherever I am — I only curled up in her chilly

bed, her muss, for a minute, just for her smell—
that her soul comes flimsily shuddering down
to settle upon my lips and limbs so

damply, awfully. You! I yell.
House mouse! Scurry, I hate
death, clingy all over me!
Squirrels, scramble
your families into the wall!
and I fight
my mother's sticky web as hard as I can for us all
until I lose, and then

when I sleep in my sweat the visitation arrives
of luminous mammal faces
and tongues, all hers.

Mooncalf, they suggest
to one another. *Prodigy. Stranger one
than strange.* They nudge
the integument curiously;
nip it, they tug
into it bit by bit, intermittently;

expose me,
lick me alive,
murmur among themselves in turn
she is what kind.

III. COMPANION ANIMAL

THEIR SKINS

It has come to him like the smell
of the pelts in the shed
picked up by a scruff of the air
and carried through the north starlight

he must decide
whether he will grow up one
of the animals or one of the men

to lie down in their clean bed
in their clean hole,
to sneak away at their first close sound to hurry home
to hate to die:

when he opens his eyes
who will have come for him

COW DREAM WITH COMMENTARY

Over at Charlie Barton's house a herd
of cows occupies the drive. The corner
vacant lot forty years ago & then Oak Street
intervene to where I see the cows from,
my first backyard. O distant indistinct
bovines, browns, Jerseys.

Your honors, we live
at last in the sources of some satisfaction,
bonnie blue, multiple green & dear hips
of the beating hillsides. One of my loves
even sleeps along next to my dream,
in the silks & favors of leniency.

Faraway some of the cows loosen, detach
to waver forwards like a heat mirage.
Likewise more, then most, drift, gradually
apportioning themselves. They populate
the lot & there they
amble & graze, tug rips in the thin weeds.

Reverences of the good evening,
do remember us to your earliest
suggestions, whom we miss. Did we do as
we were told? Sand I
heard from. Tomato rudiments. Fireflies I
consulted in my fist repeatedly.

A cow & another step down the curb
into Oak. They thud
the asphalt. Cows follow & stand in the
quiet street & turn their heads, swing tails &
visibly solemnize their ears. Two cows
heave slightly up the near curb, onto the sidewalk.

Durable powers, imaginary
these many years, detain at your pleasure
my beasts & children,
whose duties I substantially lighten for now.
I'll putter at this old shed's planks until
I've made them something else three times over.

Cows come into my yard. They pitch a bit
abruptly down the short slope. Cows straggle
mazily all the way back to where the last
ones now begin
at the beginning, but eventually
each & every one arrives, hoofs plodding up mud.

Great spirits, strict inspectors of junk &
mutilations, who
from time to time evidently stoop to
put on mere matter yourselves, I don't mind
if you do, if you crack lights from pots & pans &
tune the hemlock needles & storm the grave.

Cows fill in, lustrous cows shove all around me now,
their fragrant barrel bodies, tinged in bright breath, knock
gently & roll, hot & solid against my hands.
This is all there is,
except, possibly, the crown—
—my head, sunny among theirs.

BABY HEAD

Baby head,
you were oversleeping, I
woke you, I did, me:

only just now the
house has settled itself, and the tight
windows and the doors to rooms relax
like a fist we were in
opening up,

animals are finding their ways out,
over the roof peak
stars clear and fatten,
and the spaces
between them fill out with more stars and more spaces.

CITY LOT

Rats crouch tight
to wait out the weather. They hug their hearts
between their narrow elbows

and watch rain pick over the junk:
tug labels loose, soak down
the striped, buttoned and burst
mattresses, fill shoes, ping drums.

It never takes anything.

Sometimes they finger each other's
faces repeatedly.
Diseases line their systems and their blood goes bad.
Or they shift aside and slide their tails
loosely through glass bits,
needles, cartridges, keys.

When the sky clears big drops hang
along a steel pipe's
underside like the dugs of the stone
twins' stone wolf-mother,

                    and midafternoon
sun raises sour steam.

SCARECROW

Pitiful sticks, d'ye know me?
I hang on yr knots & nag birds.
My six dangling tin pieplates twinkle &
chime the summer's afternoon away, away,
whose trees la-di-da to high
heaven, roughage nonetheless, o
spinaches in rows.

Insolent puppies gnash my cuffs but
crosshung Jesus be my task-
master: prop me bolt upright, ripped a
bit but not down, bravely stuck this banner
morn & night to come, when, I do
believe, tormentors collapse on very bones & are
doggy poor things too.

ANIMALS BURNING

The eyes are set in their lifted heads with tongs.
They stretch, they lick
their brown flanks and catch.

Clumps of brush racing by the ocean,
crossed stalks standing all winter,
rattling fields, leaves

frittered away to ditches,
stones
be touched

by the orange flare of the animals
in procession, solemn as ancestors,
elk fire, cat fire, rabbit fire

in swelling banners, all wild:
the hunter sleeps
with his youngest son in the forest

and the bag of bodies
under steady weather,
steady wind and no strange noises.

SCRAPS

1.

Hold still, there's a
bee on the milk cup lip,
ant on the rye slice;
sister, the snake
winds up the tablecloth hem
after that song you're humming,
that food song,

          crumbs, peels.
          The trees
shake out their shade.
Mice tug the rinds off.
At the glittering thresholds
of burrow, crevice, and hole
we curl up under eyelids,
our own. We drift

           in naps
           in pouches.
Sister, tidy my dream.
We bump beside each other.
We kiss a crowded belly.
We shove for a wet nipple.
The fat world peacefully rumbles.

2.

The squirrel
cracks though to the nutmeat
which flames like a sun.
We sleep in the cheek of the afternoon.

3.

Now the ground's clean,
not a gnawed twig,
not a bitten seed.
The man tramps back and forth
poking for evidence.
He feels teeth
at his loosening nape
and at once slumps to be carried.

4.

Hush, you'll scare
the animals, she said; her hands
held applecores, peachpits, bananaskins,
green crowns of the strawberries
out to them.

PORCUPINE

Would Indian summer, untimely
hot & sluggish, never go? Shake
off persistent stolen thunder,
quit the rain? So impatiently
does the bride rehearse her regrets
that by now hysteria shrills;
she neglects lists of gifts & guests,
insists she must wear brilliant frost.

No pleasing her but that, one by one,
expectations dispel: acknowledge
no love in the black trees after all,
no love in the darkfall behind them,
& no business of love if a last,
indistinct hibernator totters
along the sidetrack, late to locate
a door of its own into the hill.

Now shuts down the shadow
economy to a standstill! nor falters
she upon homesickness, or any qualm at all
even in that certain overdelicacy
apparent among a few stars out
as lopsided November midnight
adjusts itself to face her across
the road & shirrs its quills.

MOTHS

Most of spring we kept out
apparitions by knotting
clothes' legs and arms at the doors.
Then in July the gypsy moths

found that their adult bodies hinged
matched white wings, the
tips met,
they could fly balanced

into rooms. The rooms
opened and connected and in
each one at least one
bulb light sometimes went on,

instantly filled the room up
in their weird faces, like a crash without
any harm they could tell. The
wings rocked them, steadied them

towards us, always more and more
nearly approximations
of what we meant when we
said what we did to

each other, more and more
nearly our hands as they
busied themselves
around us so commonly after all.

FLICKERS

There, a
flicker

then a second
one settle and hop a little
past us after grubs and spiders,
                              but our
attention always wanders
off things we look at,
even from two flickers' red
patches,

and I'm trying to
think of it and can't,
something I know I meant to tell you, but
only voles
keep coming and coming to mind for whatever's
left

    —they find
all those things—

until we could miss each other in the meadow,
we could turn around just past
the sumac
and call and call.

DUCKS

Maybe a murder
sucks the river's mean streak:
some melodrama underneath;
rocks waddle there in thick silt
& the slick waterlogged trees lock.

I do love a snag! —to work it all day,
to pivot up any visible debris
until the bottom drops out & the water
& mud churn; hurl it, haul it all & set it
high to dry to burn another time.

Time was I was timid, I tried
to crouch myself low in some hope
to befriend whatever might be
there timid of me. I remain pleased
to have made acquaintance.

From the bank ahead cerise bushes tip
their tips in decorum clear down. Little
April daughter, do look now &
listen!—
          wacks in preamble,
backtalk & sass.

THE WINDHORSE

for Michaela

Extravagantly dappled appaloosa-
pinto-roan in snow's
earliest dusting at bleak fall,
did your windhorse pick my woods?
So it appears. And sighs suggestively.

Maybe leafbrittle
tickles its dainty fetlocks. Or
one snow caught in a nostril, one
snow snagging at one eyelash, it shudders
glints of beatitude off its whole hide.

I do acknowledge a decent and creaturely
upbringing here on my hill.
Dying down little by little I'll
nudge to console quite beside myself
in the deep duff bed:

intercessor when the pines
careen and neigh, when the lissome
hemlocks extend their steamy necks
and the casual sovereigns
hereabouts rub them familiarly,

dispense with me to everlasting
impulse, cull me out of each
apprehension, earshot and afterthought,
to happiness kept at the ready just
so, under a flake.

WOOLEN WOLVES

The woolen wolves have fast the hills
Under their paws like loaves.
They are six of them friends.
They turn over and nose the hills.

From our houses, by the flapping clotheslines,
We watch them, two brown ones,
A red, two yellows, a white.
The hills overturn. The woolen wolves roll.

At night they sing. Their breaths sing
Down the slopes to our gardens.
The zinnias' ruffs and the lettuce
Puff up. They lift like fur.

Some days, the wolves are not there.
Clean hills, simple ones, surround our valley.
We are small as our children in blankets.
They have gone off somewhere.

JANUARY DOMESTIC

One, three of them, four;
from halfway up the path I see all five
cats-of-the-moment sprint from cover, occupy
the back porch & crouch.
Everybody turns up home now I've
arrived home too,
except the lost, who — those innumerable —
carry all this snow around in their whiskers.

Incremental aplomb over the storm door:
longest few carroty icicles fairly
clatter for me to snap them off the gutter for soup;
sunshine in them, singular blazing nutrient.
Fat years, now, since I broke
chunks of human hunger & animal into the one pot
over the blue flame.

Den fire for this evening; literature.
Two cats eye me, expressionless
ochre slits; another sits, slightly seen. Hoi polloi
hob nob in their dreams along Egyptian holy
corridors, fur rubbed
sheeny with a priests' unguent unique
to their excellencies' service,

but I still sacrifice as little as I can to you,
unbeings beseeching the ice drifts

in rigid hieratics & protocols, gloomy tunes.
I might set the shallowest dish of skim light out,
but I myself
butter a biscuit & tilt wine to commend
present company:
      long time so far & lots more
time later to bundle off missing out there.

HORSES

I was ten, I didn't call to them, they
weren't mine and didn't come.
I balanced with the split rail fence's
untidy load of yellow and white
sweet honeysuckle slung alongside,
and watched the indolent horses
drift across their paddock
always deeper into the one summer.

But for opening day of the fair they arrived
ribboned like China.
Suddenly tonight I dread my death:
I'd let tomorrow morning strap me in
the honeysuckle to be like them;
I'd sidestep and shiver while the tendrils buckled,
I'd break and run out after them forever
rollicking in air the snapped vines' ends.

SNAKE DEATH

A snake death
occurs. It does. It
continues until the snake is all dead
in its bands,

until in his kiss
testing his child's forehead when the fever breaks
a man
remembers that it happens
in his boyhood
yard not far from

here,
from the child's room, from
the hall, the stairs,
but he does not go down
any farther

while the snake's death
proceeds, all animal
and all strange to him until in his kiss

IV. SHIVER

WARD'S FIELD

Freshcut
slip of a girl &
well may you wonder:
in the upland
meadow dimming dark
fireflies' lights go hint
hint high & low,
hover, blink
out & reappear away
or near, or rise, or
sink on back
deep into high black grass.
                              Keep
wits about you, child.
Yours for the
asking be their queries all
in due time.

Slimmest spitcurl of the moon.
Up the road some, two more
trailer windows switch
on yellow, neighbors just
barely to home.
                    Overhead
bats at large

            & after you I
dance one hand appointing

stars to mark
how I have loved my life & loved
you in it. Our entirety.
       One
June evening one of the
howmany times
have I got to tell you.

APPROACH

Circle me, an ignorant grown woman among the trees.
Instill, instead of some easier one,
the lesson about the smaller animals'
modest conduct of short lives.
Each in its own sake, I mean: not its predators'. I believe
the newest-born perishing vole satisfies itself— this
particularly puzzles me.

I hope my last native visitor will be an eft.
Cold enough, alien. Exquisite prints in slick silt;
since my childhood those unmistakable two
rows of bright red-ringed-in-black spots: immaterial
as to why it abides content with itself.
Not, either, because this creature nudged a way out
of the dark-before-things-were, although it did.

Also has troubled me— there! the body language of rocks.
Greatly they resist what suffering? Between
them creeps a hidey-hole. The mineral mouth
continues so long-winded behind me that why
should anybody listen?
As if the brook water, for instance, might mutter into its
chilly fists one good reason.

NOT MOWING

All summer we didn't cut the grass.
It hunches around our legs like green cats
that vanish back into the grass.
When we turn it snags our skin, and seeds.

I've thought I must change,
learn to need less,
believe all my love so far,
let that be all.

Mice pry among
the blades, shadows of
the blades, and light.
They sit up;
their hands examine the cool stems.

Wind comes on up the road and the grass all jostles.

I could be willing to die. Even running through the yard
to tell you something that happened, I could be.

HIS EARLY WALK

Though the lake wrinkles
over light
like his eyes almost all the time

in the inseparable reeds
where some water climbs
brainstems and out to the green windy vanes
he is still peering for anything that moves,
lands or takes off.
A coarse clump
of materials keeps building in the barely visible
                        marsh verge:
                        identify us

One shout turns the hound
back from its projects to its name
which it prefers; how much more then would they
he thinks as he stands there
and spots of sun
hop like nits on the ripples,

or dreams all night how
they must haul this debris
from greater and greater distances,
how much more must they

Father, put to the air
all your finishing touches,
hands like baby birds
who startle inside your pockets
suddenly one morning among the wild blue nerves.

FLESHPOT

He trekked his body.
He pitched camp at the
bloodstream & fished there for
fishes: how they
seized on & flipped
up to his fondness,
beauties, crosshatched
all lights, colored
marmalade, tourmaline.

He's hungry. He cooks.
The thick of things
kicks in. Minutely he
pinches this &
that into the roil &
seethe to flavor the
chaos, chaos: how
much of sweet reason, rough
approximate love?

He will bed him in
luxury, vessels &
lungs. He will sleep
under his breath & dream
by leaps & bounds.
His scavengers
will tug details of
praise from the heap he will
leave them to overrun.

AUTUMNAL

Leaves asleep: the apple sequesters, peeking.
The leaves flutter, their irregular snores
rattle the wasps at death's
door where the apple's rufous luster pricks,
a little liquor swells. Much
flesh, all of it said to overween & exceed itself
for the sake of the piddling seed.

All the while they dip & snooze, the leaves mull
intense sunshine until the innocence
fumes out of it, vanishes from my song.
See, it has left us a sticky residue:
baby boys' kisses, maybe the girl's who grew
last & dropped off my hip. Oof, a vigorous
muscle tires: it was raking the bright leaves.

Spoiled husband, womanize with me tonight.
Dead to the world, the leaves hustle the dirt
road ditches & beg only to have differed
among themselves as we do. The apple collapsed
into its bruise. No, a deer took it. I wasn't
looking, the children must've stuffed an effigy.
I stayed out late in the tree wizening for you.

INDULGING AGNES

All her apples fell, and
who let that big wind out in the orchard? she howled.
Mad as a snap she was, spiteful for six hours, and it
didn't a bit of good,
busted fruits
gone to various nosy critters and all the
other mechanics of rot and spreading the seed around.

Yet well you know she herself will finger the
bruise on your latest prayer to mush, she
loves to suck any brown juice that's heartfelt
ferment; she bleats out
loud after those tainted childhoods and
marriages passing strangers toss off. How she hops and
seizes herself the corruptest part!

Challenged, she'll allow for a tolerable
fact what blotched stuff props her own house.
Whatever may quirk and quibble her taste, she's
mostly fair: years past when she first caught that tidbitten
moon smutching her girlish works she just
greeted it well well old
silvery, jollywell you too.

COSMOS

In years his tarpaper touch
makes home a quick shack. He
shocks sex & smoothes it over. His
love washes out her very child.

So she makes him this meal, it is
sliced stone, it is in jellied cold,
it is fish whites in broth the while she
stirs something else sickening

which is prayer:
                    Stars out high again,
bright heavenly bodies, burn
over my shame in your great wisps
like the whorls at human fingertips.

VALENTINE

Old rotten ice, creek's mouthful,
bless the soggy cardboard heart
of my love, this sorry condition
we're in come someday spring,
& crumple my meanest resolves

downstream to the sea of detritus
to find them a rubber boot or
such to dwell in among crustaceans &
salt themselves or pearl over or drift
at the lobster's hinge.

Our cabin annoys the very mountain! One
snowstroke more to quiet the windows, a shift
to settle the cellar heaves in justice;
so may my love's dearness to me attain
a composure beneath even the owl's notice.

I keep a box under the bed of
what-have-you for occasions:
tomorrow & tomorrow of today's
perfunctory red & lace
o make short work.

SUCCESSOR

What flesh I took pesters
to be returned, unhand
me back it
cries, plucking its lips for the
silence in the closet hung
with the other fleshes,
and for their sigh.

As for my days on this
stern earth I deny them all.

Bully for you, chick
in the deathsnest
behind my sockets,
pinfeathery with fear there and splayed
in incompetence, lunging mouth.

SHE SAYS SHE DUG UP HER DEAD CHILD

Little one I know now the grass
has your open head its own
habitually climbs the bone stairs:

All the green women
who dust night and day
who rub the ghastly knobs
and ledges until they shine
were listening for you all the time

Hug their laps
listen to the little fuss they make
over and over about you   they say

Hello you have come running
out of your bad dream
clammy sheets   shut black bedroom
thundering down the bare hall
you do not have to go back
at all

THANKSGIVING

Consider, while a meticulous wind
attends to the woods' fallen leaves,
the year's lovingkindness: November's
sky lets out the occasional
leak of light & then the pewter-
colored pond too swoons.

I announce the feast I'm giving in my body.
Even as I speak the earliest guests
arrive with the shine of the freeze on them,
frost tufts in their dark slippers,
frost at the hems & sleeves of their coats like
bushy nighttimes with big buttons.

I've not forgotten anyone,
not the single soul from longest ago
nor the soul from farthest away;
not the oldest soul, or the youngest,
or the soul from whom descend the most
generations; nor the most loved, nor the least.

BESTIAL

At the end of my life,
when I edge into marsh
where effort oozes to reeds
and the kisses of grown children
spread out like lilypads up from their long stems,

one morning a moose will stand in for my husband,
shy under its head load of politics and shock.
It steps, it snaps alders, it shoulders aside light
and muscles into the water in big marriage rings.

Quiet me then so I can watch
it wallow out:
it snuffles under and soon raises its
bulbous muzzle dangling the humid
tangles of vegetation we must have known
indelibly years
ago would be there,

and next, drawn plausibly into the slump's
some other motive,
—when the mud goes to use,
when words twitch only larvae—
grizzly old moose and I
may stare, and between us little
by little arrive at one

inane mind that remembers nothing,
until we regard each other such perfect
strangers that dread flaps up
and hies off faraway to nest
there merely its own feather.

GOOD NIGHT'S SLEEP

The night has been good all this time:
it did what it was told, & promptly;
terrible things, you have heard of some of them,
sometimes in spite of intent listening.
The good night never had to be told twice.
Can it have its sleep now? Yes.

Good night has cleaned up its room,
even the dust down the corridors sparkles!
It has laid out each of tomorrow's
lessons & necessities, you can see
your face shine up from among the implications.
Can the good night have its sleep now? Yes.

And of all sleep, there is just this one
sleep that has persevered in wait for the good night
to sift it & stir it: the sleep that was never
quite right, the one that was wrong,
the one that malingers behind as long as its long
length keeps fidgeting to rid itself of you.

Fair will be fair! Now the good night
(absent your nod, absent any late compliment)
favors its way through the nebulous clusters to this
one sleep, the one it wants to go to. Void & dispel
the last of your idling promises— all noughts— now the night
slips into the sleep that slips it free.

SHEEN

Supple summer evening rubs the house and its
figure in moon wax. Mother
wobbles at a sill there, she bears watching.

Humble River
sidles up against the acre of broken silence,
fitfully nudging along its forkful of pulp
nicked with little star lights. Might
they germinate some gloss, cast up a froth, raise nodes
that wince into us ourselves, and she none the wiser?

Trust so: she's nothing but a second
sight herself and the house like a cheesecloth
scrim that we'd see her instantly
snatch down to swathe her poor one antic in,
could she so much as guess. Sweetly
she'd begin to flirt at us, make us so sad.

But all this way she has come from her bed,
and simply set a tipsy candlepower behind her
to stay the night.

STAY

Don't you know people die all the time:
they die like the
stones turning over in
creek banks and creek beds
to turn their cold side
in,
    in November the
red oaks and red
dogwoods drop the last of their
leaves on leaves they dropped on the stones, and to
speak for the dead the leaves there this
noon said this to us:
                Stay alive for us,
                sleep with husbands and children,
                sleep with wives and children in
                real houses every night;
                all we ever
                hear is the water shiver
                on us, on us,
                maybe turn the cold side in

ABOUT THE AUTHOR

Martha Zweig has been widely published in magazines including *Prairie Schooner, Poetry, Partisan Review, Poetry Northwest,* and *Sojourner: The Women's Forum.* Her previous books include *Vinegar Bone* (Wesleyan University Press, 1999). She lives in Hardwick, Vermont.